Animals in My Yard

Chipmunks

by Christina Leaf

BELLWETHER MEDIA
MINNEAPOLIS, MN

Blastoff! Beginners are developed by literacy experts and educators to meet the needs of early readers. These engaging informational texts support young children as they begin reading about their world. Through simple language and high frequency words paired with crisp, colorful photos, Blastoff! Beginners launch young readers into the universe of independent reading.

Blastoff! Universe

Reading Level — Grade K

Grades 1-3

Grade 4

Sight Words in This Book 🔍

and	for	look	this
are	have	run	time
at	her	the	too
big	in	their	
black	is	them	
brown	long	they	

This edition first published in 2021 by Bellwether Media, Inc.

No part of this publication may be reproduced in whole or in part without written permission of the publisher. For information regarding permission, write to Bellwether Media, Inc., Attention: Permissions Department, 6012 Blue Circle Drive, Minnetonka, MN 55343.

Library of Congress Cataloging-in-Publication Data

Names: Leaf, Christina, author.
Title: Chipmunks / by Christina Leaf.
Description: Minneapolis, MN : Bellwether Media, 2021. | Series: Animals in my yard | Includes bibliographical references and index. | Audience: Grades PreK-2
Identifiers: LCCN 2020007073 (print) | LCCN 2020007074 (ebook) | ISBN 9781644873069 (library binding) | ISBN 9781681037936 (paperback) | ISBN 9781681037691 (ebook)
Subjects: LCSH: Chipmunks--Juvenile literature.
Classification: LCC QL737.R68 L428 2021 (print) | LCC QL737.R68 (ebook) | DDC 599.36/4--dc23
LC record available at https://lccn.loc.gov/2020007073
LC ebook record available at https://lccn.loc.gov/2020007074

Editor: Amy McDonald   Designer: Jeffrey Kollock

Printed in the United States of America, North Mankato, MN.

Table of Contents

Chipmunks!

Look at those
big cheeks!
Hello, chipmunk!

cheeks

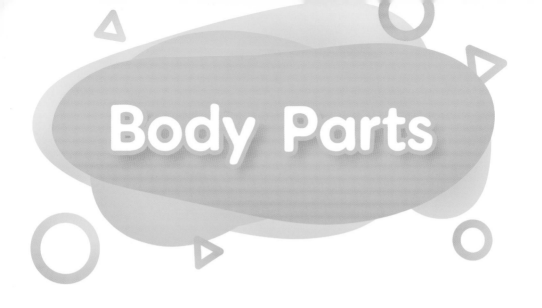

Body Parts

Chipmunks are small animals. They have long teeth.

teeth

6

Chipmunks are brown or gray. They have black **stripes**.

stripes

Their tails are long and furry.

tail

The Lives of Chipmunks

Chipmunks
are fast!
They run.
They climb trees.

Chipmunks **chirp**.
Danger is near!

Look! Seeds
and nuts.
This chipmunk
puts them
in her cheeks.

seeds

nuts

17

Chipmunks save food in **burrows**. The food is for winter.

burrow

Chipmunks sleep
in burrows, too.
Time for bed!

Chipmunk Facts

Chipmunk Body Parts

stripes

tail

cheeks

Chipmunk Food

seeds   nuts   berries

Glossary

burrows

the homes of chipmunks

chirp

to make a short, high sound

stripes

lines on a chipmunk's body

To Learn More

ON THE WEB

FACTSURFER

Factsurfer.com gives you a safe, fun way to find more information.

1. Go to www.factsurfer.com.

2. Enter "chipmunks" into the search box and click 🔍.

3. Select your book cover to see a list of related content.

Index